Scoubidou
A Book of Lanyard & Lacing

KLUTZ®

Karen Phillips

KLUTZ creates activity books and other great stuff for kids ages 3 to 103. We began our corporate life in 1977 in a garage we shared with a Chevrolet Impala. Although we've outgrown that first office, Klutz galactic headquarters remains in Palo Alto, California, and we're still staffed entirely by real human beings. For those of you who collect mission statements, here's ours:

• Create wonderful things   • Be good   • Have fun

KLUTZ®

450 Lambert Avenue
Palo Alto, CA 94306

Book printed in China. 112
Components manufactured
in China and Taiwan.

Distributed in the UK by
Scholastic UK Ltd
Westfield Road
Southam, Warwickshire
England CV47 0RA

Distributed in Australia by
Scholastic Australia Customer Service
PO Box 579
Gosford, NSW
Australia 2250

ISBN 978-1-57054-971-7

4 1 5 8 5

Write Us

We would love to hear your comments regarding this or any of our books. We have many!

Visit Our Website

You can check out all the stuff we make, find a nearby retailer, request a catalog, sign up for a newsletter, e-mail us or just goof off!

www.klutz.com

What is Scoubidou?
(Say "skoo-bee-doo")

First *it was a French pop song. In 1958 Scoubidou, the song, was such a huge hit that singer Sacha Distel became known as Mr. Scoubidou. Legend has it that one night a group of adoring fans got into his hotel room and gave him a doodad they had made out of wire insulators. They called it a scoubidou in his honor.*

Nowadays, scoubidou is the name for the hollow, plastic cord that comes with this book. All over the world, people use it to make bracelets, lanyards, key fobs, backpack danglers and more. An online search of the word scoubidou will bring up photos of some outrageously complex and time-consuming projects.

The projects in this book, on the other hand, are relatively easy and quick, perfect for scoubi newbies.

What You Get...

big beads

- Scoubidou
  - *Beads*
  - *Split rings*
  - *Lanyard clips*

small beads

toggle beads

You'll need to round up:

- *Scissors*
- *Ruler*

Also helpful:

- *Safety pin*
- *Tape*

pony beads

split rings

lanyard clips

These two scoubi colors glow in the dark!

Cool Stuff to Make

The Stretch

Before you measure and cut any scoubidou, give it a gentle stretch to get any kinks out.

Colors

The scoubidou that will show the most in a finished project is the one that requires the longest length, so make sure it's a color you like.

Tightening Knots

Keep your work secure as you go by gently tugging the scoubidou just under each knot. Don't yank too hard or the strands might stretch or even break.

Hints

Anchoring

Knotting long lengths can be much easier if you anchor one end to something you can pull against as you work. There are a couple ways to do this.

The Safety Pin System

If you're wearing jeans, you can safety pin the top loop of your project to the knee of your pants to hold it in place.

The Scoubi-Loop System

Make an anchor strand by cutting a piece of scoubidou about 18 inches (0.5 m) long. Run the strand through the top loop of your project, and then tie it around your knee, a chair, a drawer pull, a doorknob... whatever's handy.

You can use the same anchor strand over and over.

Bracelet Basics

Measuring

1. To find the perfect bracelet length for you, wrap a piece of scoubidou around your wrist without stretching it. Pinch it to mark the place where it wraps comfortably.

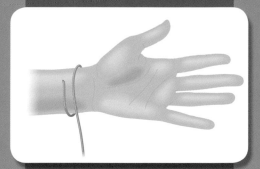

2. Measure the scoubidou from the pinched place to the end. Make your bracelets about this long.

Starting Loops

This is a ½ inch.

Scoubidou bracelets start with a simple ½-inch (1.25-cm) loop. This loop will hold the bead or knot that keeps the bracelet around your wrist, so don't make it too big. You can always stretch a small loop over a bead or knot, but you can't shrink a too-loose loop.

Fastening Bracelets

Unless you've got three hands, it can be tricky to fasten a bracelet around your own wrist. It's easiest if you have a friend put the bracelet on you.

If you're on your own, try making your hand as tiny as possible and rolling the already-fastened bracelet over it.

Zippy Wristband

What makes this wristband zippy?

It looks like a zipper and it's a zip to put together!

You'll need:

- *a 4½-foot (1.5-m) strand of scoubidou*
- *a 2-foot (0.75-m) strand of scoubidou*
- *a safety pin or scoubi loop*

1. Fold the shorter strand in half. Line up the fold with the end of the longer strand and tie them together in a simple knot, leaving a ½-inch (1.25-cm) loop at the end. Anchor the loop *(see page 6)*.

2. Weave the longest strand over one of the short strands and under the other.

3. Now head back the other way, again weaving over the closer short strand and under the farther one. Push the lacing up the side strands so the stitches are snug under the knot.

4. Keep weaving back and forth, over and under the side strands, until the wristband is as long as you want. Leave at least 3 inches (7.5 cm) of the weaving lace free at the end.

Push the stitches right up against each other so the side strands don't show.

How long should you make your wristband?

See Bracelet Basics on page 7.

5. Finish the wristband by tying all three strands in a big knot. Remove the anchor and make sure the knot is large enough to stay fastened through the loop. If it isn't, tie another knot right over the first one, making a double knot. Trim off the extra scoubi at both ends.

Lacy Bracelet

This bracelet looks especially nice with a big bead right in the center.

You'll need:

- *a 7 ½-foot (2.25-m) strand of scoubidou*
- *a 2-foot (0.75-m) strand of scoubidou*
- *a big bead (optional)*
- *a safety pin or scoubi loop*

1. Fold both strands in half and tie them together in a simple knot, leaving a ½-inch (1.25-cm) loop at the fold. Anchor the loop *(see page 6)*. Arrange the strands so the shorter ones run down the center and the longer ones are on the outside.

2. Loop the right strand behind and around the center strands and then down through the loop. Look at the picture to make sure you've got it right.

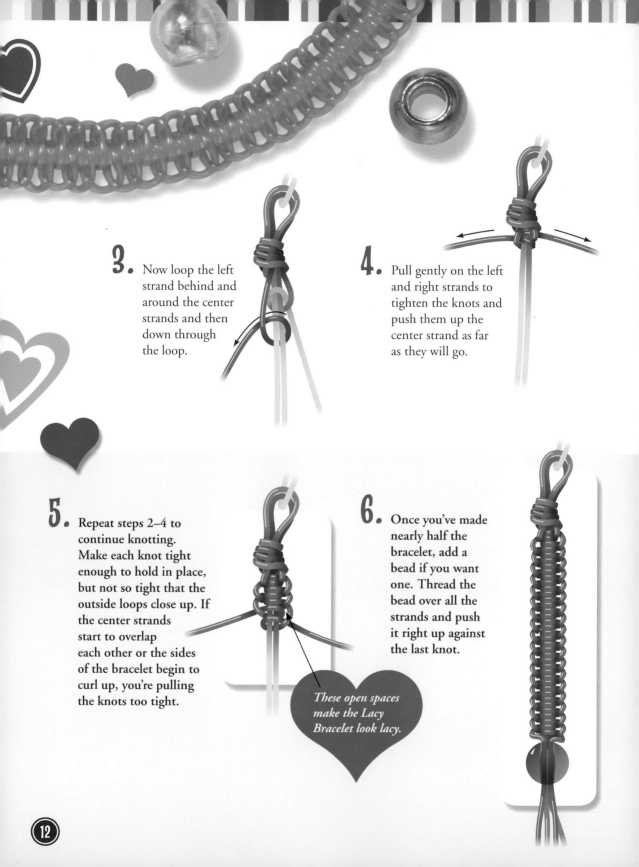

3. Now loop the left strand behind and around the center strands and then down through the loop.

4. Pull gently on the left and right strands to tighten the knots and push them up the center strand as far as they will go.

5. Repeat steps 2–4 to continue knotting. Make each knot tight enough to hold in place, but not so tight that the outside loops close up. If the center strands start to overlap each other or the sides of the bracelet begin to curl up, you're pulling the knots too tight.

These open spaces make the Lacy Bracelet look lacy.

6. Once you've made nearly half the bracelet, add a bead if you want one. Thread the bead over all the strands and push it right up against the last knot.

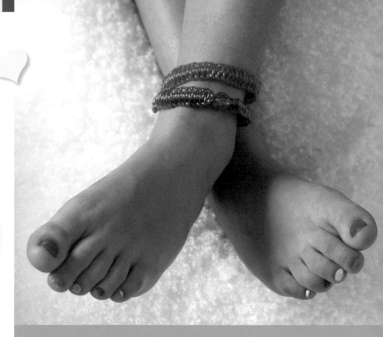

How long should you make your bracelet?

See Bracelet Basics on page 7.

To make a lacy anklet, *start with* 3 feet (1 m) *of one scoubi color and* 10 feet (3 m) *of another. Find the perfect anklet size by measuring your ankle the same way you measured your wrist* (see page 7).

7. Repeat steps 2–4 until the bracelet is as long as you want it to be.

Hold the bracelet up by the bead to make sure the two sides are the same length.

8. Tie all four strands in one big knot. Remove the anchor and check to make sure the knot is large enough to stay fastened through the loop. If it isn't, tie another knot right over the first one, making a double knot. Trim off the ends.

Fancified Flip-Flops

Use the **Lacy Bracelet knot** to give plain flip-flops scoubi style.

You'll need:

- *two 6-foot (2-m) strands of scoubidou in one color*
- *two 6-foot (2-m) strands of scoubidou in another color*
- *a pair of flip-flops*

1. Line up two different-colored strands evenly and fold them in half. Tie the strands around the toe divider so that all four ends are the same length.

2. Now you'll do the same knot as in the Lacy Bracelet. Starting with the right strap, take one of the tails and loop it from the right side, behind and around the strap, then down through the loop.

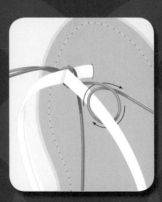

3. Now take the other tail (it should be the other color) and loop it from the left side, behind and around the strap, then down through the loop.

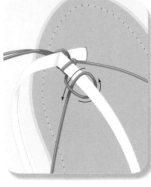

4. Repeat steps 2–3 to cover the strap. Try to keep your knots nice and even.

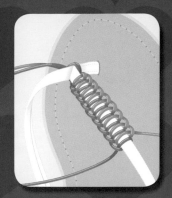

5. When you have about 2 inches (5 cm) of unlooped scoubidou left, make your last knot on the bottom side (the side closer to the sole of your flip-flop). Then bring the strand from the top side across the front of the strap and tie it to the other strand.

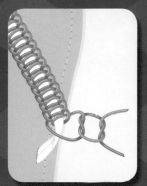

6. Tighten that last knot so it rests against the bottom edge of the strap. Trim off the excess scoubidou.

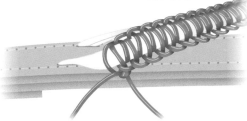

Do the same thing to the left strap, and to both straps of your other flip-flop.

When you're ready to change the look again, *just clip the scoubidou off the straps and your flip-flops are as good as new!*

Celtic Knot Wristband

It's easier to make this dramatic bracelet on a flat surface, like a desktop.

You'll need:

- *two 4½-foot (1.5-m) strands of scoubidou in different colors*
- *removable tape*

1. Line the strands up evenly and fold them both in half. Tie a simple knot about ½-inch (1.25-cm) below the fold.

2. Split the four strands into two-colored pairs. Make sure the two colors of scoubidou in each pair run side by side, not crossing over each other.

Tape this to the table.

3. Now you're going to tie a celtic knot, using each pair as one strand. Take the right pair and make a loop under the left pair.

Think of each motion as a U-turn rather than a fold.

4. Loop the left pair under the right pair...

...and then weave it through the two loops as shown.

Look at the picture to be sure you've got this right.

Tip: *If you are having trouble keeping the two colors from over-lapping, try taping each strand to its partner as you work.*

5. Before tightening the knot, slide it up the strands so it's about an inch (2.5 cm) below the starting knot. Then tighten it by tugging gently on each set of strands (first one pair and then the other) several times, adjusting the knot's position with each tug.

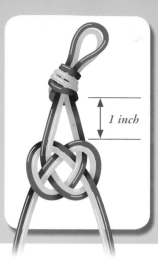

1 inch

Make sure the outside strand outlines your knot in the same color all the way around.

6. Repeat steps 3–5 to make more celtic knots, leaving about ½ inch (1.25 cm) between them.

5 knots: *a snug fit*
6 knots: *a semi-snug fit*
7 knots: *a loose fit*

The knotted wristband will want to twist in the middle. That's okay — it'll straighten out once it's around your wrist.

7. Finish up by tying all four strands into one big knot that is large enough to stay fastened through the loop. If it isn't, tie another knot right over the first one, making a double knot. Trim off the extra scoubi.

Wrapped Pen

Give your pen a cool look and a great grip by wrapping it in scoubi stripes.

You'll need:

- *two* 4-foot (1.25-m) *strands of scoubidou*
- *a pony bead*
- *a pen*

1. Tie one of the strands of scoubi around the pen, near the writing end. Tighten the knot, leaving a 2-inch (5-cm) tail.

2. Tie the second strand right below the first strand, covering the tail end. Be sure to leave a 2-inch (5-cm) tail on the second strand, too.

3. With the first strand, make a loop on the left side of the pen. Now wrap this same strand around the pen and up through that loop. Be sure the wrapped strand covers both tail ends but leaves the other long strand free. Pull the knot snug.

Keep this strand up and out of the way.

4. Next, loop the second strand on the left, wrap it around the pen and pull it up through the loop. Cover the two tail ends but leave the other long strand free.

No matter how your pen rotates, the loop still goes on the left.

5. Loop and wrap both colors one more time each and then carefully clip off the tail ends.

Clip here.

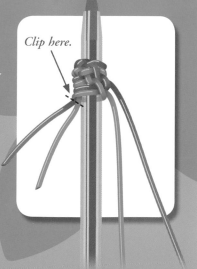

6. Keep looping and wrapping, alternating strands. The knots will start to spiral around the pen as you go.

Each pair of knots goes in front of the last one.

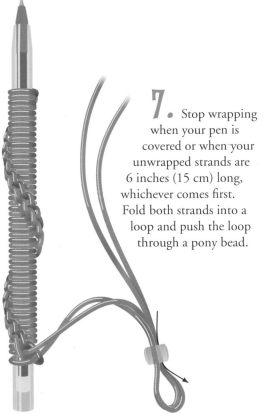

7. Stop wrapping when your pen is covered or when your unwrapped strands are 6 inches (15 cm) long, whichever comes first. Fold both strands into a loop and push the loop through a pony bead.

8. Tie the ends in a tight knot.

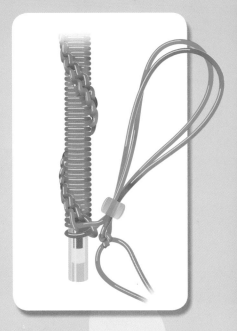

9. Slide the bead over the knot, as snug against the pen as possible. Clip off the ends.

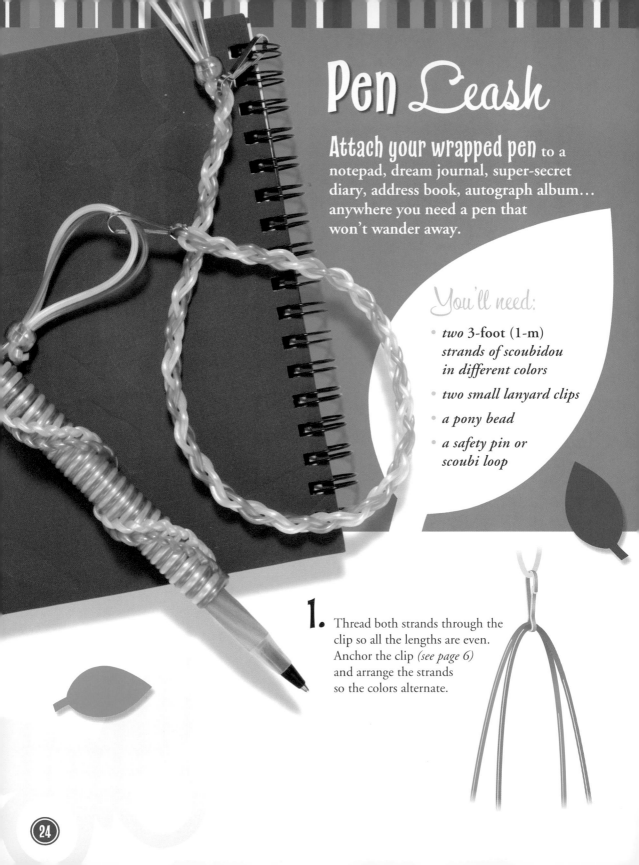

Pen Leash

Attach your wrapped pen to a notepad, dream journal, super-secret diary, address book, autograph album... anywhere you need a pen that won't wander away.

You'll need:

- *two 3-foot (1-m) strands of scoubidou in different colors*
- *two small lanyard clips*
- *a pony bead*
- *a safety pin or scoubi loop*

1. Thread both strands through the clip so all the lengths are even. Anchor the clip *(see page 6)* and arrange the strands so the colors alternate.

2. Now you'll start making a swirly braid. Cross the outside right strand under the two inside strands…

…and then back to the right over the nearest strand.

3. Now fold the outside left strand under the two inside strands…

…then back to the left over the nearest strand.

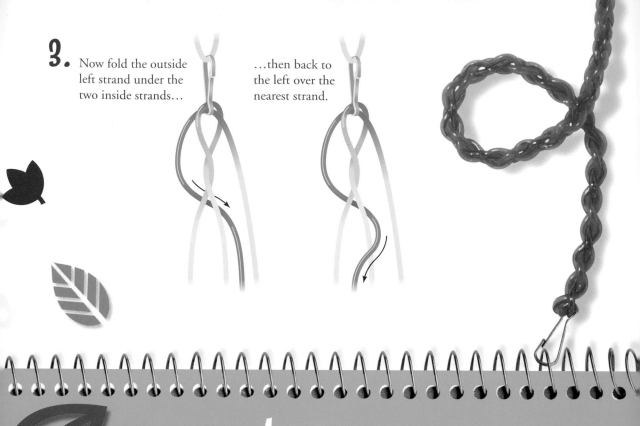

4. Gently pull the strands so the braid tightens up near the clip. Keep repeating steps 2–3 to continue the swirly braid.

The colors should start to form a swirl pattern, like a peppermint stick.

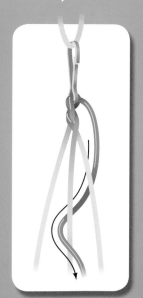

5. Once your braid is about 11 inches (28 cm) long, tie the strands of one color together. Then tie the strands of the other color together.

6. Slide a pony bead up all four strands so it covers the knots. Slide a second clip through the braid right next to the bead, catching a strand of each color. Trim off the excess lacing, leaving a 2-inch (5-cm) tail.

7. Attach the tail end of the leash to your notepad…

…and clip the other end through the loop on your pen.

Write on!

Spiral Bracelet

This bracelet looks kind of like a textbook illustration of DNA.

But pretty.

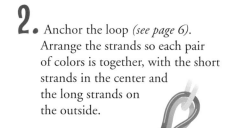

You'll need:

- *two 5½-foot (1.5-m) strands of scoubidou*
- *a pony bead*
- *a safety pin or scoubi loop*

1. Line up the strands evenly and fold them together so one side is 1 foot (0.25 m) long and the other side is 4½ feet (1.5 m) long. Tie the strands in a simple knot, leaving a ½-inch (1.25-cm) loop at the fold.

2. Anchor the loop *(see page 6)*. Arrange the strands so each pair of colors is together, with the short strands in the center and the long strands on the outside.

3. Cross the outside left strand over the center strands and under the outside right strand, leaving a loop to the left.

4. Pass the right strand under the center strands and up through the loop you made.

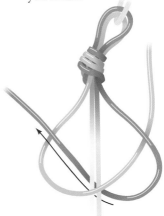

5. Pull both outside strands to secure the knot. Tighten the knot just enough to hold it in place.

If you pull the knots too tight, the bracelet won't spiral.

6. Repeat steps 3–5 to continue making knots, always crossing the left strand in front of the center, and the right strand behind the center. The knots will naturally start to spiral around the bracelet as you go. Every now and then, go ahead and let the bracelet rotate the way it wants to.

Don't pull the knots super tight.

7. Make your bracelet as long as you want it, leaving at least 3 inches (7.5 cm) of scoubidou free at the end, and then slide a pony bead up over all four strands so it rests against the bottom of the last knot. Tie the strands together in one big knot to hold the bead in place. Trim off the ends.

How long should you make your bracelet?
See Bracelet Basics on page 7.

Loopy Hair Elastic

These scoubified hair elastics are surprisingly stretchy and hold hair beautifully.

You'll need:

- a hair elastic
- a 4-foot (1.25-m) strand of scoubidou

1. Fold the scoubidou so one side is 4 inches (10 cm) long. Hold the fold against the side of the hair elastic as shown.

Look for fabric-covered elastic ponytail holders — *ideally, the kind with no metal parts.*

2. Thread both the long and short ends under the elastic and through the loop.

Pull the ends so the loop is snug around the elastic. You've just made a **lark's knot.**

3. Now make an underhand loop: Thread the long strand under and around the elastic, and then down through the loop.

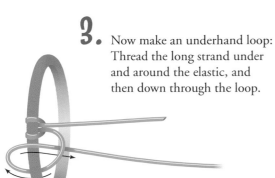

Pull the scoubidou snug.

4. Next, an overhand loop: Thread the long strand over and around the elastic, and then up through the loop.

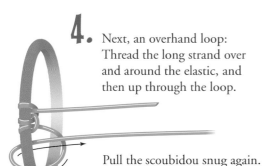

Pull the scoubidou snug again.

5. Repeat steps 3–4, alternating underhand and overhand loops, all the way around the elastic. Push the loops up the elastic, close to each other, as you go.

underhand loop: under *the elastic* **and** down *through the loop*

overhand loop: over *the elastic* **and** up *through the loop*

6. When you've got about 4 inches (10 cm) of unlooped scoubidou left, tie it securely to the 4-inch length where you started.

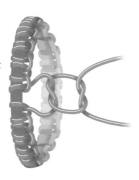

Clip off the ends.

Loop de Loopy
Hair Elastic

If you've successfully made a Loopy Hair Elastic, **you're ready to tackle the Loop de Loopy.**

You'll need:
- *a hair elastic*
- *two 4-foot (1.25-m) strands of scoubidou in different colors*

1. Fold one of the strands so one side is 4 inches (10 cm) long. Start with a lark's knot, just as you did in steps 1–2 on page 32.

2. Fold the other strand the same way, but this time put the loop on the left side, just below the first strand. Pull the ends through in a lark's knot.

Don't tighten this knot.

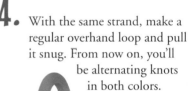

3. Now make an underhand loop that links the upper and lower strands together:

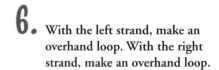

Thread the long top strand under the elastic, up through the lower lark's knot and down through the new upper loop.

Pull both knots snug.

4. With the same strand, make a regular overhand loop and pull it snug. From now on, you'll be alternating knots in both colors.

5. With the left strand, make an underhand loop. With the right strand, make an underhand loop.

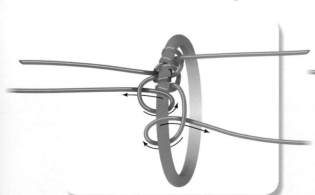

6. With the left strand, make an overhand loop. With the right strand, make an overhand loop.

7. Repeat steps 5–6 all the way around the elastic. Every now and then, push the loops up the elastic so they are close together.

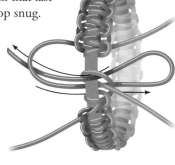

8. When you've got about 4 inches (10 cm) of unlooped scoubidou left, end with a special underhand loop: under the elastic, up through the very first lark's knot and down through the loop. Pull that last loop snug.

9. Tie the strands of one color together in a secure knot. Then tie the strands of the other color together. Clip off the ends.

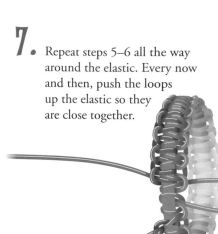

You'll need:

- a split ring
- a 3-foot (1-m) strand of scoubidou in one color
- a 1½-foot (0.5-m) strand of scoubidou in another color
- a big bead
- a safety pin or scoubi loop

Woven Whatzit

It's a key ring! Or a backpack charm... or a zipper pull... or a belt-loop dangler...

Whatever it is, everyone needs at least one.

1. Anchor the split ring *(see page 6)* and run the short strand through it so the ends are even.

2. Run the long length through the ring and line it up so one end is even with the two short strands. Tie all the strands together in a simple knot close to the ring.

Making the Woven Whatzit *is a lot like making the Zippy Wristband (page 8), except now you're weaving through three strands instead of two.*

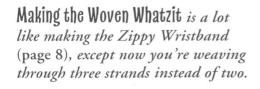

3. Arrange the three even lengths so the matching colors are on the outside. Weave the long length under one outside strand, over the middle strand and under the other outside strand.

4. Now head back the other way, this time weaving over the near outside strand, under the middle strand and over the far outside strand.

Push the lacing up the center strands so the stitches are tight against each other.

5. Repeat steps 3–4 to keep weaving through the three even strands. This may look like kind of a mess for the first few stitches. Just push the stitches tight against each other and it'll start to look better soon.

Remember: *Alternate under-over-under and over-under-over.*

6. Once the woven part is about 2½ inches (6.5 cm) long, slide a big bead over all four strands so it's right up against the bottom of the woven section.

7. Tie all four strands in a simple knot to hold the bead in place. Trim the ends to any length you like.

Toggle Bracelet

This delicate-looking bracelet is named
for the special bead that fastens it around your wrist.

1. Fold the short strand so
one side is 12 inches
(30 cm) long and the
other side is 6 inches
(15 cm) long. Tie the
very middle of the long
strand around the short
strand about ½ inch
(1.25 cm) below the
fold. Anchor the loop
(see page 6).

*Make sure the outside
strands are about the
same length.*

You'll need:

- *a 1½-foot (0.5-m)
  strand of scoubidou*
- *a 4½-foot (1.5-m)
  strand of scoubidou*
- *4 small beads*
- *a toggle bead*
- *a safety pin or scoubi loop*
- *removable tape*

2. Now you'll start
making square
knots: Cross the
left strand over
the two center
strands and
under the far
right strand,
leaving a loop
on the left side.

3. Cross the right
strand under
the middle
strands and up
through the
loop you made
on the left.

Pull both
outside strands
to tighten this
left knot.

4. Now do the same thing on the right side: Cross the right strand over the two center strands and under the far left strand, leaving a loop on the right side.

5. Cross the left strand under the middle strands and up through the right loop. Pull this **right knot** snug.

left knot
+ right knot
──────────
square knot

6. Repeat steps 2–5 five more times, so you have a total of six square knots.

bump

Hint: *If you can't remember where to start your next knot, look at the last knot you tied. If the little bump is on the left, start your next knot on the left. If the bump is on the right, start on the right.*

7. Carefully clip off the shorter center strand up close to the last knot. Slide a small bead up the remaining center strand.

8. Now make four more square knots beneath the bead.

9. Add a bead and four more square knots. Then add a third bead and another four square knots.

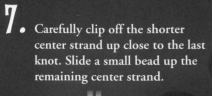

10. Thread a fourth small bead on the center strand. Then thread the toggle bead, but don't slide it all the way up the strand. The distance from the top loop to the toggle bead should match your perfect bracelet length *(see page 7)*.

11. Fold up the part of the center strand that comes after the toggle bead. Use a little tape near the toggle bead to hold it in place.

12. Tie six square knots over both the center strand and the taped-up tail, removing the tape after the first square knot is complete.

pull to shorten

pull to lengthen

Now remove the anchor and check the bracelet length around your wrist. You can adjust it by pulling gently on the toggle loop or on the extra center strand.

13. Once you're happy with the length, securely tie the long strands together on the underside of your bracelet and trim off the ends. Clip off the extra center lacing.

Beautiful!

To fasten the bracelet, *rotate the toggle bead so it points into the loop and push it completely through.*

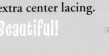

Classic Lifeguard Lanyard

A lifeguard would use this handy overhead lanyard to wear a whistle around her neck. **It's a great way to keep whatever you need hanging around.**

This is an advanced project. Go slow and be patient!

1. Anchor the clip *(see page 6)* and center your scoubidou on it. Arrange the colors exactly as shown.

Make all four strands the same length.

2. Now you'll start making the diamond braid: Cross the right strand under the two inside strands and then back to the right over the nearest strand.

Note: *The diamond braid works just like the swirly braid that makes up the Pen Leash (see page 24). The only difference is the order in which you arrange the colors at the very beginning.*

44

3. Cross the outside left strand under the two inside strands and then back to the left over the nearest strand. Pull the strands tight.

4. Repeat steps 2–3 until the braid is about 32 inches (81 cm) long. It has to be long enough to slip over your head when the two ends are joined.

braid this one next

TIP: *If you have to leave your scoubidou before you're finished, tape the strands down on a piece of paper in the right order.*

If they get mixed up anyway, pull both strands of one color to the left and the other two strands to the right. Now look at the outside strands. Whichever is highest is the one you start with next.

5. The next step is to change from the diamond braid to the box knot. Start by tying the two inside strands together.

This is a good time to remove the anchor loop.

6. Arrange your scoubidou so it looks like the illustration: strands of one color pointing away from you and toward you, and strands of the other color pointing left and right. They may not do this naturally, and it may not look too neat, but don't worry about it.

7. Start a box knot by folding the top strand down and the bottom strand up.

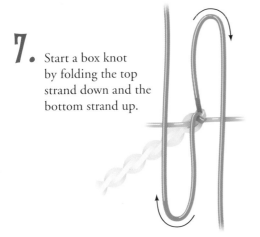

8. Then weave the left lace over the nearest strand and through the far loop…

9. …and weave the right lace over its nearest strand and through the far loop.

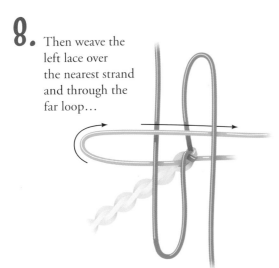

10. Gently tug on each strand, one after another, to tighten the knot.

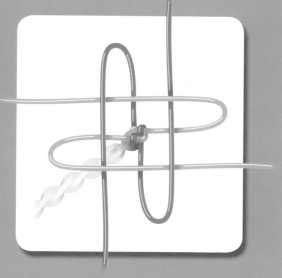

11. Make another box knot in just the same way, but this time do not tighten it. Be sure the strands still form the shape of a box, even though it is loose.

12. Poke the clip right up through the center of this knot and pull through about 3 inches (7.5 cm) of finished diamond braid. Then make the box knot snug around the braid.

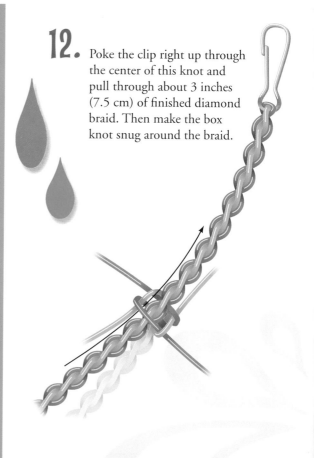

13. Continue making box knots **around** the diamond braid until about an inch (2.5 cm) of the braid is all boxed up. Pull the box knots tight enough to stay securely in place, but not so tight that they squish the diamond-braid out of shape.

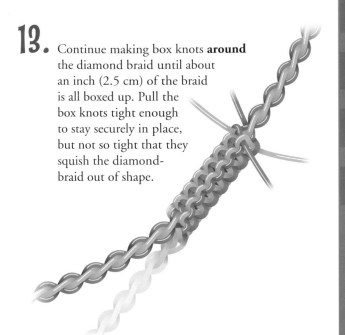

14. To end the box knots, you have to tie a special finishing knot. First, make sure your scoubidou looks exactly like the illustration. If it doesn't, make another box knot. Leave your last knot a little looser than usual.

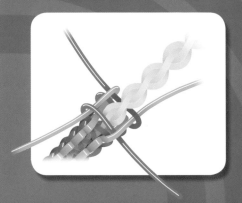

Next you'll go counter-clockwise around the braid, wrapping each strand under its neighbor and up into the center of the knot. The loops will always go under a strand of the other color and pull up inside a strand of the matching color. Keep reading for the step-by-step.

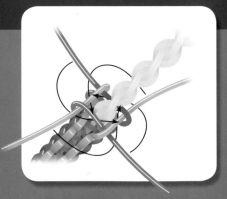

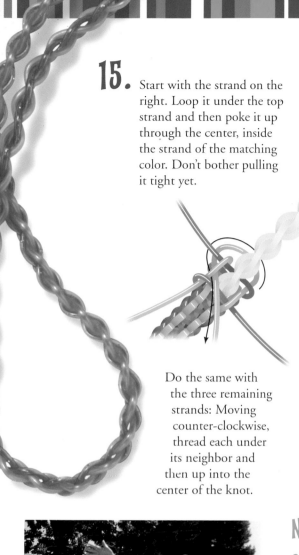

15.
Start with the strand on the right. Loop it under the top strand and then poke it up through the center, inside the strand of the matching color. Don't bother pulling it tight yet.

Do the same with the three remaining strands: Moving counter-clockwise, thread each under its neighbor and then up into the center of the knot.

16.
When all the strands have been pulled through the knot, hold the box knots in one hand and pull each loose end tight with the other. Trim the ends at angles to any length you like.

When your lanyard is complete, you can adjust the size by pulling the diamond braid through the box knots.

Now make a splash in style!

To clip on a lip balm, *give it the Wrapped Pen treatment* (see page 20).

You'll need:

- *two 3½-foot (1.25-m) strands of scoubidou in different colors*
- *a split ring*
- *a safety pin or scoubi loop*

Wrist Lanyard

This is a stylish, scaled-down version of the Classic Lifeguard Lanyard.

Make it with the split ring if you want a handy key chain.

1. Using a split ring in place of the lanyard clip, follow steps 1–3 on pages 44 and 45. Work the diamond braid until it is about 11½ inches (29 cm) long.

2. Continue with steps 5–16 to finish up. Once you're done, pull the diamond braid through the box knots to adjust the fit around your wrist.

Can't get enough?

Here are some simple ways to keep the Klutz coming.

1 Order more of the supplies that came with this book at klutz.com. It's quick, it's easy and, seriously, where else are you going to find this exact stuff?

2 Get your hands on a copy of **The Klutz Catalog**. To request a free copy of our mail order catalog, go to klutz.com/catalog.

3 Become a **Klutz Insider** and get e-mail about new releases, special offers, contests, games, goofiness and who-knows-what-all. If you're a grown-up who wants to receive e-mail from Klutz, head to klutz.com/insider.

If any of this sounds good to you, but you don't feel like going online right now, just give us a call at 1-800-737-4123. We'd love to hear from you.

Bead Loom Bracelets

The 15 Greatest Board Games in the World

Capsters™

Paper Fashions Fancy

Crochet

It's All About Me!

Friendship Bracelets

Just Between Us

Picture Bracelets

My All-Time Top 5

My Style Studio

Credits

designer
April Chorba

art director
Kate Paddock

production coordinator
Patty Morris

project consultant
(flip-flops, hair elastics, toggle bracelet, wrapped pen and leash)
Julie Collings

technical illustrators
John & Judy Waller

photographers
Melissa Barnes, Peter Fox
Joseph Quever

production editor **Jen Mills**

scoubi-don't **John Cassidy**

models

Laurel Anderson
Katya Austin
Talia Bakker
Mira Bertsch
Chloe Blanchard
MacKenzie
    Bontempo
Brianna Boyd
Nora Boyd
Becca Brown
Flora Cabili
Leigh Ann
    Cannon
Clara Chang
Emily Colvin
Devin Daugherty
Megan Davis
Helen Gonzalez

Sam Herzog
Kelly Hoover
Ariella Jensen
Alyssa Kelly
Lori Krakirian
Jerusha Krebs
Lauren Latterell
Sydnie Lee
Megan Lok
Priscilla Lok
Maev Lowe
Valerie Makovkin
Ekekela Novero
Catherine Partain
Collene Roe
Emily Saunders
Savannah-Rose
    Soutas

Kimberly Starnes
Gabriella Trujillo
E. L. Tucher
Kayla Valpey
Dominique
    Wegmueller
Samantha
    Whitford
Nicole Whitson
Zoe Zaorski
Camillle Simone
    Zolopa

doggie divas

Tini Chorba
Maisy Moon

Show Us Your Genius

Send us a photo of your coolest scoubidou creation and it may get displayed on the Fridge of Fame at klutz.com. That's world-wide recognition! To learn more, visit klutz.com or e-mail us at **thefridge@klutz.com**.

special thanks to:

Laurie Bryan
Debra Myers
Mark Phillips
Debby Shannahan
    & Ron Moon
Jill Turney
AMF Redwood Lanes

Cal Skate of Milpitas
College Terrace Library
Golfland USA,
    Sunnyvale
Laurel Anderson and
    all the scoubi-testers
    at Klutz